God is Listening

33 Days of Praying with Scriptures

Cunningham Family,

Continue to allow the Lord God to use you for His glory! Keep the Faith!

By

Nartarsha Michele Davis

Love,

Nartarsha Michele

2/11/18

ISBN-13: 978-1977713131
ISBN-10: 1977713130

God is Listening

DEDICATION

TO GOD BE THE GLORY!

This book is dedicated to the many women and men, boys and girls, reading this. It is for you who are brave enough, and yet humble enough to admit, you still need God to listen to you, within every moment of your lives. My prayer is that you will feel God's amazing touch, and see Him in the many miracles around you.

God is Listening

CONTENTS

God is Listening

ACKNOWLEDGMENTS

It is with deep gratitude that I thank God for the soft whispers, and loud trombones of speaking to my heart. He truly knows His child, and what I needed in order to push me further, into His great plans.

I thank and truly appreciate my husband, and my Masterpiece, Rev. John Paul, for encouraging and inspiring me in this journey. Thank you for listening to my long speeches, and conversing with me, about the God plans.

To my four amazing children, Jehromie, Jordan, Neyah, and Natalie, thank you for your stories, which are continuing to unfold. God knew what He was doing when He brought each one of you into my life, and I thank God for doing it. All of you are so special to me, and will forever hold your own special place within my heart, no matter what happens!

To my beautiful and astonishing "MAMA", thank you for encouraging me with your words of love, actions of love, unconditional love, and support. You are truly, A WOMAN OF GOD!

Thank you to my one and only blood sister, Natalie. You are a wise, woman beyond your years. Thank you, for your "pearls of wisdom," that you would often drop around the family gatherings.

Thank you to my Pastor, Dr. Ralph D. West, Sr ., and Lady Sheretta West. You both are such a huge inspiration to me, and I am grateful to God for sending my husband and I, to serve under your committed leadership, at The Church Without Walls.

To Rev. Dr. Jewel M. London, thank you for pushing me to always become better for God. I appreciate our conversations of motivation, and your prayers. Thank you for paving the way for me in my calling, and letting the light of God shine, like the 'Jewel', you are.

To all of my encouragers, supporters, and my Superstars, who have given of your heart, time, finances, and self-sacrifices, thank you so much!!

May God continually bless each and every one of you, abundantly above all, you could ever think or imagine, in Jesus' name, amen!!

1
SUNDAY

WEEK 1

Philippians 1:5-6 New International Version (NIV)

5 because of your partnership in the gospel from the first day
until now, 6 being confident of this, that he who began a good work in you will carry it on to completion until the day of Christ Jesus.

Father God, thank you for the good news that we have as believers. Thank you for sending your son, Christ Jesus to walk this earth for thirty three years, and minister humbly to those who needed to feel your love. Thank you for the ultimate sacrifice in Christ Jesus, who showed us over and over again how to carry out your good works. Lord God, you are so faithful to put in us what we need, and faithful to help us complete what we need to do. Thank you for not leaving us alone, but for actually being our partner, so that we can do what it is you have ultimately called us to do. Thank you for your covenant promise, and salvation in Jesus' name, amen!

WEEK 2

Psalm 3:2-4 New International Version (NIV)

2 Many are saying of me,

"God will not deliver him."[a]

3 But you, Lord, are a shield around me,

my glory, the One who lifts my head high.

4 I call out to the Lord,

and he answers me from his holy mountain.

Father God, thank you for being our protection. Thank you, for being our shield from the hands of our enemies. Thank you for sustaining us, keeping us, and guiding us in your righteous way. We called out to you Lord God, so many times, and you answered us in so many ways. Thank you, being gracious and loving enough to love us beyond ourselves. Thank you for lifting us up in you, Father God, so that we can continue to give you all the glory and honor, in Jesus name, amen!

WEEK 3

Psalm 46:1 MSG

[A Song of the Sons of Korah] God is a safe place to hide, ready to help when we need him. We stand fearless at the cliff-edge of doom, courageous in seastorm and earthquake, Before the rush and roar of oceans, the tremors that shift mountains. Jacob-wrestling God fights for us, God-of-Angel-Armies protects us.

Father God, you are almighty, and ready to save us, from the dangers and snares of this world. Thank you for being our protector, strength, and putting in us, what we need at all times. Thank you Father God that we don't have to fight our battles, because you care for us, and we need only to have faith, and trust in your word. Thank you Lord God, for being all powerful, & omniscient. In Jesus' name, amen!

WEEK 4

Acts 2:25 King James Version (KJV)

25 For David speaketh concerning him, I foresaw the Lord always before my face, for he is on my right hand, that I should not be moved:

Father God, thank you for always being available to us, never leaving nor forsaking us. I bless your Holy name for all that you are. Thank you for being with me through all the dangers in this life, spiritually and physically. I will not be moved because you are with me, in Jesus' name, amen!

Prayer Notes:

2
MONDAY

WEEK 1

Joshua 24:15 New King James Version (NKJV)

15 And if it seems evil to you to serve the Lord, choose for yourselves this day whom you will serve, whether the gods which your fathers served that were on the other side of the River, or the gods of the Amorites, in whose land you dwell. But as for me and my house, we will serve the Lord."

Lord God, thank you for being who you are. Thank you for being so omniscient that you have allowed all people to serve you, Father. Lord God, I bring my life, family, and home, under your complete authority. I want to serve you, with my whole being. No matter who, or what anyone else is serving, I humbly submit and give my all to you. You know what is best for us, and I trust you Lord God. Thank you for the privilege to be able to serve you. In Jesus' name, amen!

WEEK 2

1 John 4:8 New King James Version (NKJV)

8 He who does not love does not know God, for God is love.

Father God, thank you for being love, so that we can know how to love. Thank you for loving us unconditionally, without restraints. Thank you, for being you, Father God. For you are God, and you are love. If there is anything that is within me, that does not show love, I ask that you would help me Lord God, and show me how to love. If there is anything that is not right in your eyes, please purify me, Oh Lord. Help me to love freely, and without judgment. In Jesus' name, amen!

WEEK 3

Psalm 92:5-8 Holman Christian Standard Bible (HCSB)

5 How magnificent are Your works, Lord,

how profound Your thoughts!

6 A stupid person does not know,

a fool does not understand this:

7 though the wicked sprout like grass

and all evildoers flourish,

they will be eternally destroyed.

8 But You, Lord, are exalted forever.

Father God, thank you for being magnificent, and blessing us abundantly above all that we can ever ask or think of. You know us better than we know ourselves. Your thoughts towards us, your creation, are good thoughts. Thank you for being all that you are! Lord God, You sent your son, Christ Jesus to show us love unconditionally, and we bless your Holy name for this! We thank you for showing us these things, and you being with us, allowing your Holy Spirit to dwell within us, we can become more Christ-like, and not an evil-doer. We don't want to be stupid, nor foolish, but want to have good thoughts, and praise you forevermore! You are most worthy of all our praise, and we magnify you, Lord God! In Jesus' name, Amen!

WEEK 4

Romans 8:32-34 New International Version (NIV)

32 He who did not spare his own Son, but gave him up for
us all—how will he not also, along with him, graciously give us
all things? 33 Who will bring any charge against those whom
God has chosen? It is God who justifies. 34 Who then is the
one who condemns? No one. Christ Jesus who died—more

than that, who was raised to life—is at the right hand of God and is also interceding for us.

Father God, we thank you for sending your one and only son to live and die, for us. Thank you for being so loving towards us and being love. Thank you for giving us what we need, and working on our behalf. You, Lord God are almighty, and we thank you for choosing us, and also justifying us. In Jesus' name, amen!

Prayer Notes:

___

___

___

___

___

___

___

3
TUESDAY

WEEK 1

The Lord will fulfill His purpose for me. Lord, Your love is eternal; do not abandon the work of Your hands.

Psalm 138:8 Holman Christian Standard Bible (HCSB)

Lord God, you are Holy, and we praise you for who you are. We ask that you will forgive us of our sins, and anything that is not pleasing in your sight. Thank you for blessing us, with your divine purpose. You have shown us love by first loving us, and being love to us through your son, Jesus Christ, and we are forever grateful. We ask that you Father God, would continue to protect and keep us and our families, never leaving us, nor forsaking us, as you promised in your Holy word. In Jesus' name, we pray, Amen!

WEEK 2

2 Kings 20:2-5 Holman Christian Standard Bible (HCSB)

2 Then Hezekiah turned his face to the wall and prayed to the Lord, 3 "Please Lord, remember how I have walked before You faithfully and wholeheartedly and have done what pleases You." And Hezekiah wept bitterly.

4 Isaiah had not yet gone out of the inner courtyard when the word of the Lord came to him: 5 "Go back and tell Hezekiah, the leader of My people, 'This is what the Lord God of your ancestor David says: I have heard your prayer; I have seen your tears. Look, I will heal you. On the third day from now you will go up to the Lord's temple.

Father God, we thank you for allowing us to be able to come to you wholeheartedly and cry out to you. We thank you that you hear us, oh Lord, and always answer our prayers right on time. What you promised and established in your word, you remember, and you do not forget your faithful servants. Thank you, for being loving, and keeping your promises to us, your people. We bless you, Abba God, in Jesus' name, Amen!

WEEK 3

1 Thessalonians 5:9-11

Holman Christian Standard Bible (HCSB)

9 For God did not appoint us to wrath, but to obtain salvation through our Lord Jesus Christ, 10 who died for us, so that

whether we are awake or asleep, we will live together with Him.
11 Therefore encourage one another and build each other up as
you are already doing.

Thank you, Father God, for not holding anger over our heads, and for loving us instead. Thank you, for the eternal promise, that we as believers in Jesus Christ, have a life with you. We will continue to help one another, and to remind them of this promise, you have given to your children. In Jesus' name we pray, Amen!

WEEK 4

1 John 1:8-10 New International Version (NIV)

8 If we claim to be without sin, we deceive ourselves and the
truth is not in us. 9 If we confess our sins, he is faithful and just
and will forgive us our sins and purify us from all
unrighteousness. 10 If we claim we have not sinned, we make
him out to be a liar and his word is not in us.

Father God, thank you for caring for us, keeping us, and guiding our steps. Thank you for caring so much for us that you sent your only son, Jesus Christ to us, so that we can be saved if we believe he died on the cross, was buried, and rose again three days later for our sins to be forgiven. Thank you that we can confess our sins unto you, and we can be forgiven, and redeemed by the blood of Jesus. You, Lord God are such a loving, and forgiving God, and for that we are grateful. Hallelujah, and In Jesus' name, amen!

Prayer Notes:

4
WEDNESDAY

WEEK 1

Psalm 145:8-12 New International Version (NIV)

8 The Lord is gracious and compassionate,

slow to anger and rich in love. 9 The Lord is good to all;

he has compassion on all he has made. 10 All your works
praise you, Lord; your faithful people extol you. 11 They tell of
the glory of your kingdom and speak of your might, 12 so that
all people may know of your mighty acts and the glorious
splendor of your kingdom.

Thank you Father God, for being good and gracious toward us. We praise you and lift up your Holy name. Please forgive us of our sins, and anything that is not pleasing in your sight, Lord God. Help us to continue to be faithful to you, as we tell of all of your goodness which you have bestowed upon us. Bless you Lord God, in Jesus' name, we pray, Amen!

WEEK 2

Matthew 17:19-21 New King James Version (NKJV)

19 Then the disciples came to Jesus privately and said, "Why could we not cast it out?"

20 So Jesus said to them, "Because of your unbelief;[a] for assuredly, I say to you, if you have faith as a mustard seed, you will say to this mountain, 'Move from here to there,' and it will move; and nothing will be impossible for you. 21 However, this kind does not go out except by prayer and fasting."[b]

Father God, we come to you thanking you for showing us your mighty, and miraculous power. Thank you for showing us how to have the same power, through prayer and fasting. You told us that if we have faith, and not huge faith, but just a little mustard seed of faith, we can do mighty things in this world. We can speak, just as you did, and things will begin to move, and change. Lord God, you said we could cast out those things that are demonic and evil, in Jesus name! You have given us all that we need, and all we have to do is have FAITH. So, Abba Father, I ask that if you see in me where I lack the faith I need to have, help me. Help me to have that mustard seed faith, so I can do miraculous signs and wonders for your glory. In Jesus' name, Amen!

WEEK 3

Psalm 33:18-19 Holman Christian Standard Bible (HCSB)

18
Now the eye of the Lord is on those who fear Him—
those who depend on His faithful love
19
to deliver them from death
and to keep them alive in famine.

Lord God, you are faithful, and for this we thank you. You are so faithful that your love endures throughout many generations, and forevermore. We are grateful that we can put our hope and trust in you, oh Lord. For you, are the one on whom we can depend, to keep us from the flaming arrows of the enemy. Thank you, for keeping us, and shielding us. Thank you, for providing for us in our times of not only our needs, but even in some of our wants. You are faithful, Lord God, and for this, again we say thank you. In Jesus' name we pray, Amen!

WEEK 4

Psalm 119:57-60 English Standard Version (ESV)
57
The Lord is my portion;
I promise to keep your words.
58
I entreat your favor with all my heart;
be gracious to me according to your promise.

59
When I think on my ways,
I turn my feet to your testimonies;
60
I hasten and do not delay
to keep your commandments.

Oh Holy and Gracious God, thank you for being my portion and being a covenant keeper. Thank you, for blessing me with your favor. You are so worthy of all my praise, and I lift up your Holy name. I worship and adore you, for you are good. You are great. You are my all and all. You have given me so many good things which outweigh, the bad things. Father God, thank you for all that you have done for my family, and I. Thank you that I can look ahead, and know that if you blessed me before, you can bless me again. I look to you for your teachings and obey your words so that I can be in your perfect will, and not your permissive will. Thank you for your word, which keeps me protected, and blessed. In Jesus' name, Amen!

Prayer Notes:

5
THURSDAY

WEEK 1

1 Peter 2:9-10 New King James Version (NKJV)
9 But you *are* a chosen generation, a royal priesthood, a holy
nation, His own special people, that you may proclaim the
praises of Him who called you out of darkness into His
marvelous light; 10 who once *were* not a people but *are* now the
people of God, who had not obtained mercy but now have
obtained mercy.

Lord God, thank you for choosing and considering me, your royal priesthood. Thank you for calling me out of the wilderness, into something greater. Thank you for calling me out of the dark into your magnificent light. Thank you for being a light shining through me into this dark world, so that others may see you, and not me. Abba Father, please continue to bless my walk, as I continue on this journey in your Holy word. Keep me close to you, so that I will not stray from your radiant glory. I want to be encompassed by your power. Fill me up with your glorious power, so much that it attracts those that need to be saved by your son, Christ Jesus. Thank you for granting me your mercy. You are so good, and worthy to be praised. In Jesus name, Amen!

WEEK 2

Psalm 37:5 English Standard Version (ESV)

5

Commit your way to the Lord;

trust in him, and he will act.

Father God, I ask that you forgive me for falling short with you. I ask for your forgiveness of my sins. Thank you for new beginnings, and commitments. Thank you for trusting me, and blessing me with all which has been placed in my hands. Lord God, I commit it all to you, because I trust in your word, and your ways. I ask that you will help me to always fulfill your perfect plan, according to your perfect, and not permissive will. Help me, to hold tighter to your hand, and continue to keep you first, in everything I do. You are faithful in keeping your word, and I believe you will act on your word. Thank you for being faithful. In Jesus' name I pray, Amen!

WEEK 3

Matthew 8:24-27 English Standard Version (ESV)

24 And behold, there arose a great storm on the sea, so that the boat was being swamped by the waves; but he was

asleep.25 And they went and woke him, saying, "Save us, Lord; we are perishing." 26 And he said to them, "Why are you afraid, O you of little faith?" Then he rose and rebuked the winds and the sea, and there was a great calm. 27 And the men marveled, saying, "What sort of man is this, that even winds and sea obey him?"

Lord God, please forgive us of our sins. We come humbly asking you to please cover, and protect the many people of the many cities which are affected by the storm. Please bless the many people who are putting their lives on the line to help rescue those in need, as well as the many other volunteers. Please bless each and every person, and family, who are going through this difficult time, in exceeding & abundant ways. For everything that is lost during this time, we ask that you would not only replace it, but give blessings beyond measure. Please keep our minds in perfect peace, reminding us of your promise, to never leave us, nor forsake us. Although it is heartbreaking and sad times, we believe that even this, will work for the good of those who love you Lord God, as you promised in your word. Thank you for your Holy Word, to remind, and refresh us when we are weary. Thank you for your son, Jesus Christ, and it is in Jesus' name we pray, Amen!

WEEK 4

1 Corinthians 6:19-20 Holman Christian Standard Bible (HCSB)

19 Don't you know that your body is a sanctuary of the Holy Spirit who is in you, whom you have from God? You are not your own, 20 for you were bought at a price. Therefore glorify God in your body.[a]

Father God, thank you for blessing me with a body that is equipped with all that I need, because you have blessed accordingly. Thank you for the presence of the Holy Spirit dwelling within me, and being my comforter as I walk through this thing called, life. Help me to always remember, to not do anything outside of your perfect will, which could go against my life, body, or you Father God. I ask that you will always be with me. Help me to have confidence in you, so that I will love my body, keep it healthy, and pleasing in your sight. Help me to keep focus to have a healthy lifestyle, honoring you with my body and life. Thank you for sending your son to live and die, on the cross for my sins, and rising again, in order that I may live in this temporal body now, and a heavenly body later. give you all the glory, and honor, Lord God. In Jesus' name, Amen!

Prayer Notes:

____

____

____

____

____

6
FRIDAY

WEEK 1

1 Corinthians 1:9 New King James Version (NKJV)

9 God is faithful, by whom you were called into the fellowship of His Son, Jesus Christ our Lord.

Lord God, you are so faithful and worthy of all my praise. Thank you, for being who you are, and being faithful towards me. You have been with me, protecting me, and keeping me even when I didn't want to be kept. Thank you for your faithfulness. It is what I need from day to day, as I go about in this world of uncertainty. I know I can depend on you being faithful to me and all that I am involved with. Thank you, for showing your love by sending your son, Jesus Christ to us, to save us. Thank you Jesus for being faithful to our Father God, and showing us how to be faithful, by your perfect example. Even when it was hard, and you wanted to give up, you pressed on and stayed faithful. Jesus, it wasn't easy for you to pray, and ask that the cup to be passed from you, while you were in the

Garden of Gethsemane, but you pressed on, and prayed, 'not your will, but God's will be done. Thank you for staying faithful, and a covenant keeper. In Jesus' name, Amen!

WEEK 2

2 Timothy 3:12 King James Version (KJV)

12 Yea, and all that will live godly in Christ Jesus shall suffer persecution.

Father God, thank you for your son, Jesus Christ. Thank you for sending him as the ultimate sacrifice for us, so that we as your people, can have everlasting life. We know that because we will have everlasting life, with you, there are some things which we must go through while we are here in this world. Just as your son suffered, we being in the Holy family, must also suffer. But we hold on to the promises of your Holy word, which lets us know that our suffering is only for a little while. We know that we have the victory through your son, Christ Jesus. So while the suffering does not feel good, we know it is for the ultimate good. We believe by faith, that we are more than conquerors, and as your word says, the just shall live by faith. When we get weak, Father God, help us to hold fast to your promises. We really do want to live a Godly life for you, and your glory. In Jesus' name we pray, Amen!

WEEK 3

Psalm 23 King James Version (KJV)

23 The Lord is my shepherd; I shall not want.

2 He maketh me to lie down in green pastures: he leadeth me beside the still waters.

3 He restoreth my soul: he leadeth me in the paths of righteousness for his name's sake.

4 Yea, though I walk through the valley of the shadow of death, I will fear no evil: for thou art with me; thy rod and thy staff they comfort me.

5 Thou preparest a table before me in the presence of mine enemies: thou anointest my head with oil; my cup runneth over.

6 Surely goodness and mercy shall follow me all the days of my life: and I will dwell in the house of the Lord for ever.

Oh Holy God, thank you for being my shepherd, and blessing me with all I need. Thank you for going before me, and preparing the way for me. Thank you for your goodness and mercy, that you don't have to give, but you do, just because you are good, and you are God. Thank you Lord! You are so worthy of all my praise, and I worship your Holy name! Lord God, you know exactly when I need to rest, and when I need to rise. You give me just the right portion of rest, and for that I am grateful. When my soul is weary, you restore me. Thank you Father God! You are so good. There are some places, that I may enter, and evil is all around, but God! You have kept me, from the hand of my enemies. You have and continue to bless me abundantly, even in the presence of my enemies. Thank you for being so good, and looking out for me. Thank you for being my comforter, protector, and provider. Lord God, please continue to show me your grace and mercy, never leaving me, and never forsaking me, as you promised in your Holy scriptures. Again, I say thank you for following me, as well as going before me all the days of my life. Thank you for the anointing on my life, as well as your guidance with your anointing. In Jesus' name, I pray, Amen!

WEEK 4

Deuteronomy 13:4 New King James Version (NKJV)

4 You shall walk after the Lord your God and fear Him, and keep His commandments and obey His voice; you shall serve Him and hold fast to Him.

Lord God, you are good and worthy of all my praises. You know what is good for me, and have given commandments for my good. You knew me before I knew myself. So Father God, I trust you, and will walk in line with your perfect word, for my life. You have given specific instructions for me to obey you, because you know what is best. When I hear your voice, I will obey your word. When I read your word, I will walk your word. It may be difficult at times, for me to serve you with my whole heart, and my whole life because of my flesh. However, you know my desire is to serve and honor you, wholeheartedly. Keep me close to you Lord God, and I will hold fast to your word, being the best that I know how to be. I want to honor you with my whole life. I want to be your great servant Lord God. I want to be obedient to you. I know that obedience is better than any sacrifice I could ever offer up to you. When I am obedient, you are a great rewarder of it. You know the perfect reason, for my perfect obedience. You know the many blessings which will come out of my obedience to your word, and I believe you will honor your word. Thank you for your faithfulness to your covenant. Thank you for trusting me to be used as a vessel to show your obedience. Again, I say you are good and worthy of all my praises. I will serve you Abba, and hold fast to your perfect word. In Jesus' name, I pray, Amen!

Prayer Notes:

____

____

____

____

____

7
SATURDAY

WEEK 1

Proverbs 18:1-2 New International Version (NIV)

An unfriendly person pursues selfish ends
and against all sound judgment starts quarrels.

2 Fools find no pleasure in understanding
but delight in airing their own opinions.

Lord God, thank you for blessing me with a sound mind, and a good heart. Thank you for instilling in me your Holy Spirit, which allows me to seek after being self-less, instead of being self-ish. I ask that when my flesh rises up, and wants to be an unfriendly person, you would keep me focused on your good word. Keep me in sync with the Holy Spirit, to be loving even to those who are unloveable, and kind to all people. We are not called to be an island among ourselves, as you state in your word, but called to help others. Help me to always seek after the good. Help me to understand others, and listen to wise and sound judgement, in order that I may be in harmony with them. Lord God, my flesh does get weak, and there are times that I don't want to listen to understand, and only want to speak about my issues. But Abba, help me to give these issues over to you, and lay them at your feet. Help me to have the ear to listen with love and not hurt. Thank you for being able to open up to you, and give you my problems, cares, and concerns. Thank you for showing me how to be a good friend to others. Thank you for showing me how to love. In Jesus' name, I pray, Amen.

WEEK 2

Matthew 6:31-33 The Message (MSG)

30-33 "If God gives such attention to the appearance of wildflowers—most of which are never even seen—don't you think he'll attend to you, take pride in you, do his best for you? What I'm trying to do here is to get you to relax, to not be so preoccupied with getting, so you can respond to God's giving. People who don't know God and the way he works fuss over these things, but you know both God and how he works. Steep your life in God-reality, God-initiative, God-provisions. Don't worry about missing out. You'll find all your everyday human concerns will be met.

Father God, you are miraculous in your works! You are such an on time God. You know what we need, when we need it, and how we need it. Thank you, for being faithful to your word, and to us. Thank you, for caring, and being concerned, about every detail of our lives. Thank you, for always providing for our needs. Thank you, for answering our concerns, even before we know they are a concern. You are such an amazing God. Even when we have health problems, financial concerns, family issues, relationship drama, personal tragedies, you are with us, and comforting us with your Holy Spirit. You have provided all that I have needed, and I am grateful. I trust and believe that if you take care of the animals and plants in your creation, then surely we as humans being a bigger part of your creation, will be taken care of. I know that it may not always be on my time, but it's in your perfect time. My faith in you, will keep me putting you first, in everything I do. For I know that if I seek after you, I have everything I need. You are a great God, and I love you Lord, God. In Jesus' name, I pray, Amen!

WEEK 3

Psalm 71:24 New King James Version (NKJV)

My tongue also shall talk of Your righteousness all the day long;
For they are confounded,
For they are brought to shame
Who seek my hurt.

Thank you, for being my rock and redeemer. You are so good to me, and I will praise you, forevermore. You are righteous, and worthy of all my worship. With my lips, I will continue to tell of all your goodness, and how you saved me. Thank you, Lord God, for saving me from the fiery darts of my enemies. Thank you, for saving me from the burning pits of hell. You are so good to me, and I will praise you, forevermore. Thank you, for your hedge of protection which surrounds me, all the days of my life. Thank you, for confusing those who try to bring me down, and put me to shame. Thank you, for putting my enemies to shame. Thank you, for upholding your word and promise. You are so good to me, and I will praise you, forevermore. In Jesus' name, I pray, Amen!

WEEK 4

Hebrews 2:17-18 New International Version (NIV)

17 For this reason he had to be made like them,[a] fully human in every way, in order that he might become a merciful and faithful high priest in service to God, and that he might make atonement for the sins of the people. 18 Because he himself suffered when he was tempted, he is able to help those who are being tempted.

Father God, you are omnipotent, and we thank you for being the God you are. You knew that we were going to be faced with difficult things, and would need to be reminded about your son, Jesus Christ's suffering. Thank you, for giving us the strength. Thank you, for sending witnesses to testify to which they have suffered, and yet survived and even thrived. Thank you for doing the best thing you could have ever done. You sent your son, Jesus Christ to endure, and go through criticism, mistreatment, trials, floggings, and even death, all with strength. Even in what Jesus thought was His weakest moment, actually was his strongest moment, because he relied completely on you Father God. You gave him, His ultimate strength. Thank you, Abba God, for raising Jesus, our savior up from the dead, and allowing him to make atonement for our sins. Thank you, for loving us so much that you wanted to save us from the dying world. In Jesus' name, I pray, Amen!

Prayer Notes:

____

____

____

____

____

____

____

8
SPIRITUAL WARFARE

Ephesians 6:11-18 New King James Version (NKJV)

11 Put on the whole armor of God, that you may be able to stand against the wiles of the devil. 12 For we do not wrestle against flesh and blood, but against principalities, against powers, against the rulers of the darkness of this age,[a] against spiritual hosts of wickedness in the heavenly places.13 Therefore take up the whole armor of God, that you may be able to withstand in the evil day, and having done all, to stand.

14 Stand therefore, having girded your waist with truth, having put on the breastplate of righteousness, 15 and having shod your feet with the preparation of the gospel of peace; 16 above all, taking the shield of faith with which you will be able to quench all the fiery darts of the wicked one. 17 And take the helmet of salvation, and the sword of the Spirit, which is the word of God; 18 praying always with all prayer and supplication

in the Spirit, being watchful to this end with all perseverance and supplication for all the saints.

Father God, we come to you, praising you for who you are. We thank you for your magnificent power. We come right now confessing our sins unto you Father God, and ask that you would forgive us of anything that is not right within your eyes. Forgive us, Father God, for any unrighteousness, & uncleanliness. We ask in the name of Jesus, that you would cleanse us right now, Lord God. Straighten us up, Lord God. Straighten us out, Lord God. We thank you for your son Jesus, who walked this earth with authority from you Father God. Lord God, you showed us, told us, and still are telling us in your word, how to be strong in you Lord, and in your MIGHTY power. Thank you for telling us the real clothes we are to put on daily, & not any worldly name brand line of clothing. You said we are to put on our spiritual clothes, better known as the FULL armor of you, Lord God;

-the belt of truth buckled around our waist,

-the breastplate of righteousness in its right place,

-the gospel of peace for our feet.

-the shield of faith, so we can extinguish ALL the flaming arrows of the evil one.

-the helmet of salvation

-the sword of the Spirit, which is your Holy word that will accomplish what is has been set out to do, and will not return unto you void.

Thank you For your reminder that our struggle is not against flesh and blood, but against the rulers, against the authorities, against the powers of this dark world and against the spiritual forces of evil, in the heavenly realms. And so we CANNOT, and would be foolish to think we can fight this spiritual battle without the spiritual clothing you HAVE equipped us with. Thank you Father God, for allowing us access and giving us the authority to be able to pray in season, and out of season; when the sun is shining, and when it is night; when we have earthquakes, hurricanes, turmoil, trials and tribulations. Thank you Father God, that you have given us authority, and tongues to speak, to those things that are coming up against us, your people, and your kingdom work, in Jesus' name!! We cast all of these situations, and all of our anxieties, unto you Father God, because you truly do care for us, and in just the RIGHT season, not PAST season, just the right time, and NOT in overtime, you will lift us up!!

Now, Abba Father, we ask that you would let your light shine so brightly through us that, your presence is felt when we encounter other people, & that we light up this dark world, with your Holy Spirit. Please continue to do a work within us, that will seep out of the seams, spilling onto others, that they will see your joy, goodness, and mercy. And when you bring those people across our paths, that don't know your son Jesus Christ, for themselves, and are not saved, let them see us, shining so brightly that they come to us being attracted to YOUR illuminating, and ever glowing light, and ask what must they do to be saved.

Thank you, for being God, and we claim all of these petitions in victory through your son, our savior, Jesus Christ, amen!

Prayer Notes:

____

____

____

____

____

____

____

9
CHILDREN

Luke 18:15-16 The Message (MSG)
15-16 People brought babies to Jesus, hoping he might touch them. When the disciples saw it, they shooed them off. Jesus called them back. "Let these children alone. Don't get between them and me. These children are the kingdom's pride and joy.

Lord God, you are so loving towards us to not only send your son Christ Jesus, to us. But you also, showed us love through you loving the children. Lord God, you said that our children are a blessing to us, and the world. Thank you, for blessing us with children around us, in families, churches, and our communities. We ask that you will cover them with your hedge of protection, and keep them safe from the hand of the enemy. Allow your love to always flow from us as parents, mentors, coaches, or family members, to the children. Let them feel your presence, as they get closer to you, Lord God. Please help them to always remember that even though they are in the world, they are not to be of the world. Remind them daily of how precious they are, and as you said in your word, the kingdom's pride and joy. Thank you Jesus, for calling and claiming our children back to you, even when others try to keep them away. Lord God, your word and ways are loving, and powerful, and we thank you, for your tender care and concern.

In Jesus' name, Amen!

Prayer Notes:

____

____

____

____

____

____

____

10

*Marriage *1 *2 *3*

Ephesians 5:19-21Holman Christian Standard Bible (HCSB)
19 speaking to one another
in psalms, hymns, and spiritual songs,
singing and making music
from your heart to the Lord,
20 giving thanks always for everything
to God the Father
in the name of our Lord Jesus Christ,
21 submitting to one another
in the fear of Christ.

Prayer 1: Father God, thank you for bringing my spouse into my life. Thank you for considering me, and choosing the best spouse for me. Help me to always speak with love, honor, and respect towards my spouse. Help me to keep my tone in an understanding way, so that my words will always have the melody of your Holy Spirit flowing along the notes of my speech to my spouse. Father God, please cover my covenant marriage with your abundant blessings of joy and peace. Let my spouse and I always enjoy one another, and be thankful for each other, through the good times, and the bad times. When my spouse and I come to the times of misunderstanding, or misinterpreting, help us to be able to come together on one accord, submitting to one another out reverence for you. Help us to overcome the trials, tribulations, and any turmoil, we may face. Abba Father, when we go through the fiery trials, bond us closer together, and bind us in your Holy word. We thank you in advance for covering us, and keeping our marriage together on the solid rock of Jesus! In Jesus' name, I pray, Amen!

Prayer 2: Lord God, thank you for my marriage, as well as the many other marriages in the world. You showed my spouse and I how to become as one, in your word, and through your word. I ask that you would always give me a heart for my spouse. Give me a passion for my spouse. Give me a hope for my marriage. When moments of heartaches come in our marriage, I ask that you would give my spouse and I, the desire to calmly speak to each other. Allow us to see each other as you see us, and not as each other's enemies. Bind us closer to each other. Connect our hearts, and souls to each other, as we connect closer to you, Lord God. Be with my spouse as we are apart from each other. Please give my spouse favor, as they are working on their jobs today. Let your Holy Spirit fall fresh on them, so that they will feel your presence. Allow your presence to be sensed in and through them, so that others in their workplace may also see you, Father God, shining through them. Please provide my spouse the peace needed to be able to work efficiently, diligently, and calmly. I ask for traveling grace, for my spouse, as they travel to and from their workplace. Please cover the vehicle which is being driven by my spouse. I thank you in advance that no weapon formed against my spouse, shall ever prosper, In Jesus' name. Thank you for the victory of success, promotion, and favor in my spouse's life. Thank you for allowing me to be my spouse's prayer partner for life, and until death do us part. In Jesus' name, Amen!

Prayer 3: Gracious, and Eternal God, thank you for this moment of prayer I have with you. I ask that you would forgive me for not always being kind towards my spouse. Forgive me for being short tempered, and not always being the best spouse I can be. Help me to overcome any strongholds, I have against my spouse, or my marriage in Jesus' name. Help me to be sensitive to the Holy Spirit, in my marriage, so that I can serve my spouse, and not myself. Help me to focus on being more self-less, and not self-ish. Help me to become closer to my spouse, and fulfill the needs of my spouse. I know I cannot do it all, Lord God. I cannot do it by myself. But, with you, Lord God, I can do all things which strengthens me. So I ask you to please help me to become a better spouse. Where I am weak, help me to become stronger. Where I am too prideful, humble me, so that you can lift me, as well as my marriage up, in you Abba God.

Thank you, for your help. Thank you, for the repair and restoration, of my heart and marriage. In Jesus' name, I pray, Amen!

Prayer Notes:

Prayer Notes:

ABOUT THE AUTHOR

Nartarsha Michele Davis, is passionate about God's word, and believes in the power of prayer. She is married, the mother of four children, and grandmother of two glamourous girls. She resides in Houston, TX, where she is a friend, and mentor to those persons whom God, has called her to. She is a Cosmetology Instructor, and owns her own salon business of twenty years, Super Star Stylists Beauty Spa, located in Cypress, TX. Nartarsha, is a faithful member of The Church Without Walls, in Houston, TX. She along with her husband, currently serve as Marriage Ministry Coordinators, within the church as well. Together they have founded, and are directors of Family Affair Ministries, LLC. Nartarsha, has also accepted, and is fulfilling her calling of Preaching the Gospel, of Jesus Christ. She is available to go where God sends her to speak, teach, and preach the Gospel.

Please share with the author, any testimonies or miracles, you experienced from God, after praying during these 33 days.

Nartarsha Michele Davis

Family Affair Ministries, LLC
PO Box 2211
Cypress, TX 77410
USA

nartarsha@familyAministries.com

familyAministries@gmail.com

www.familyAministries.com

Facebook: @nartarshamicheledavis